Happy Birthday to

Good Books™

Intercourse, PA 17534
800/762-7171 • www.goodbks.com

Text by Lois Rock
Illustrations copyright © 2002 Gabriella Buckingham
Original edition published in English under the title
Now You Are 3 by Lion Publishing, plc, Oxford, England.
Copyright © Lion Publishing 2002.

North American edition published by Good Books, 2002.
All rights reserved.

NOW YOU ARE 3
Copyright © 2002 by Good Books, Intercourse, PA 17534
International Standard Book Number: 1-56148-396-6
Library of Congress Catalog Card Number: 2002024141

Printed and bound in Singapore.

Library of Congress Cataloging-in-Publication Data
Rock, Lois
 Now you are 3 / Lois Rock, Gabriella Buckingham.
  p. cm.
 Originally published: Oxford, England : Lion Pub., 2002.
 Summary: Three-year-olds spend their birthdays dressing, eating, playing,
sleeping, and resting.
ISBN 1-56148-396-6
 [1. Birthdays--Fiction. 2. Toddlers--Fiction. 3. Stories in rhyme.] I. Title:
Now you are three. II. Buckingham, Gabriella. III. Title.
PZ8.3.R58615 Nn 2002
[E]--dc21   2002024141

Last year, little darling,
you would stay
quite close to me...

But now you do things
by yourself, for this year

you are

3

Here's a birthday
message from
the golden shining sun:
welcome to another year
of happiness and fun.

Head and shoulders,

knees and toes,

can you put on
all your clothes?

A knife and a fork,
let's sit and talk...

A silver spoon,
let's go out soon.

Monday is
a busy day

and Tuesday's
busy, too.

Wednesday makes
me weary for
there's such a lot to do...

Thursday is a thinking day

and Friday's full of fun.

Then all at once it's Saturday:
the weekend has begun...

Sunday is for sleeping late
and spending all the day

in quiet rest and thankfulness
till sunlight slips away.

The spring of the year –
it is yellow and green.

The trees grow their leaves
and the flowers are seen...

Summer brings sunshine
and clear skies of blue.
The days are so long
and there's so much to do...

Autumn is misty,
the leaves turn to red,
and morning dew sparkles
on each spider's web...

Winter grows colder
with frost and with snow.
Through the bare branches
the chilly winds blow.

Climb a silver ladder
to the moon above.
Pick a bowl of starlight
for the one you love.